© 2024-2025 Chelsea Kong

All rights reserved. All images used in this book are licensed copies from their respectful owners including Canva, Unsplash, 3D Artist, AI Image Gen, others. This book or any portion thereof may not be reproduced or used in any manner whatsoever without the express written permission of the publisher except for the use of brief quotations in a book review.

Printed in 2024-2026, Made in Toronto, Canada
ISBN: 978-1-998335-40-4
Hard Cover Book ISBN: 978-1-998335-70-1
Library and Archives Canada

They must tell the truth and show proof about what they share in court.
The judge can choose to give more time.
They will give a new court date.

A plea can be called a petition. He must sign it, and the advocate will give a copy of to the judge before the court date.

A law clerk helps a lawyer or advocate. The judge has an assistant who takes notes of all the court cases and the judge reviews. When a case is on, it is called a court hearing.

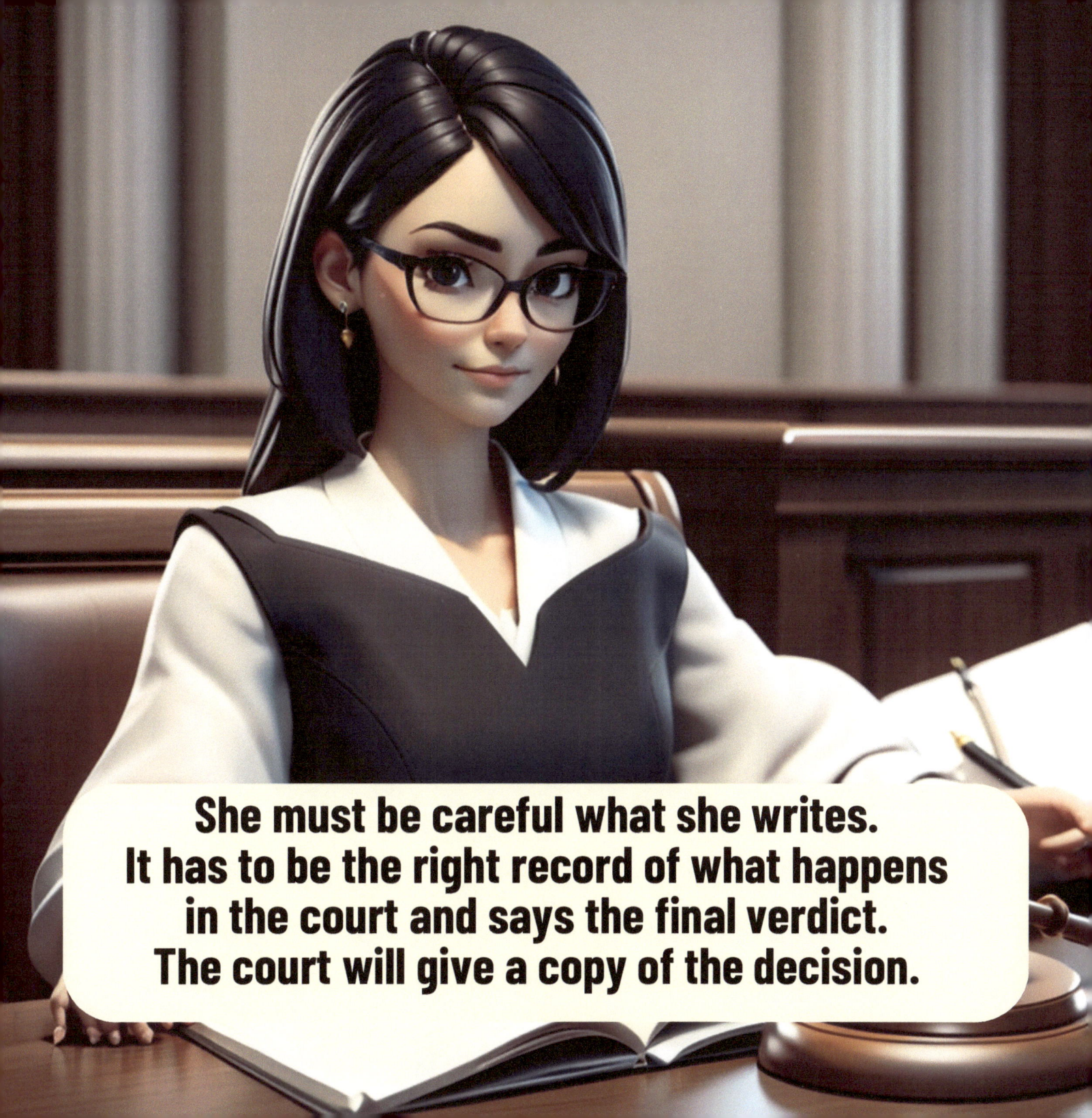

The judge makes a choice from the case.
Some cases are worse than others.
Police may be there in the room too.

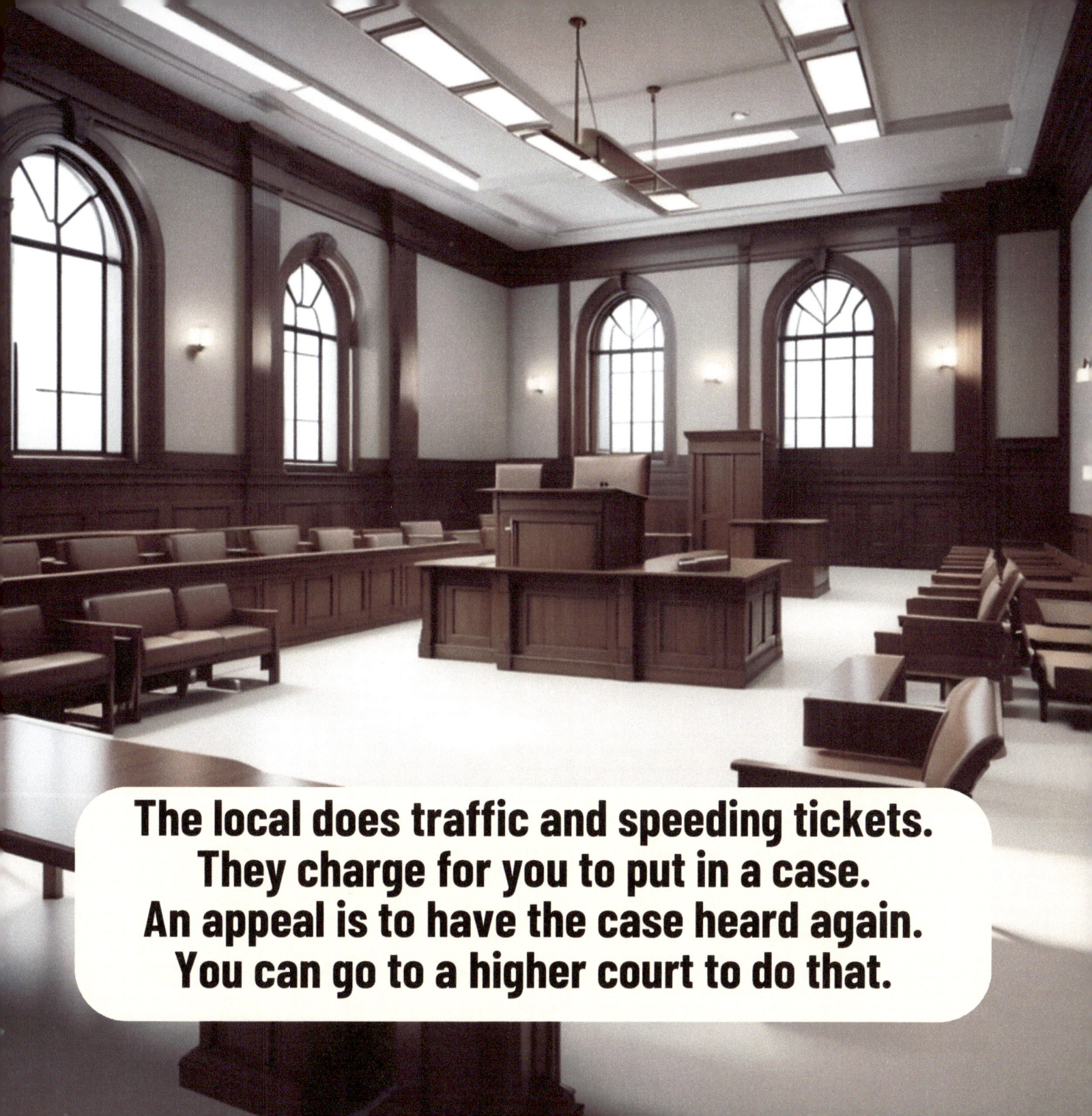

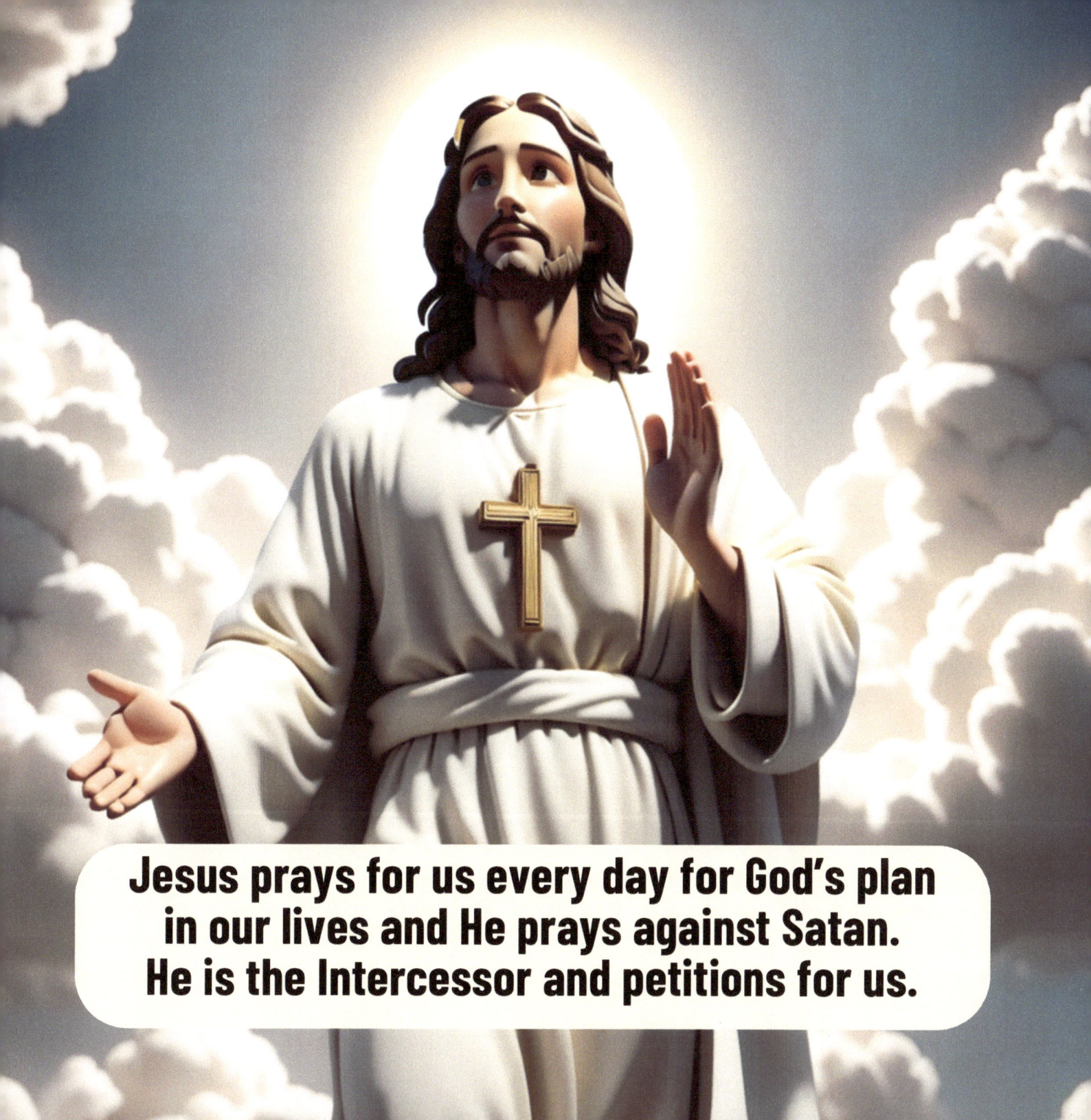

King Solomon came before the Lord after he gave sacrifice offerings. He put the Ark of the Covenant inside Solomon's Temple.

The Lord will let us into the Inner Court.
Then into the Holy of Holies
in the heavenly Tabernacle.
He talks to us there and we must listen.

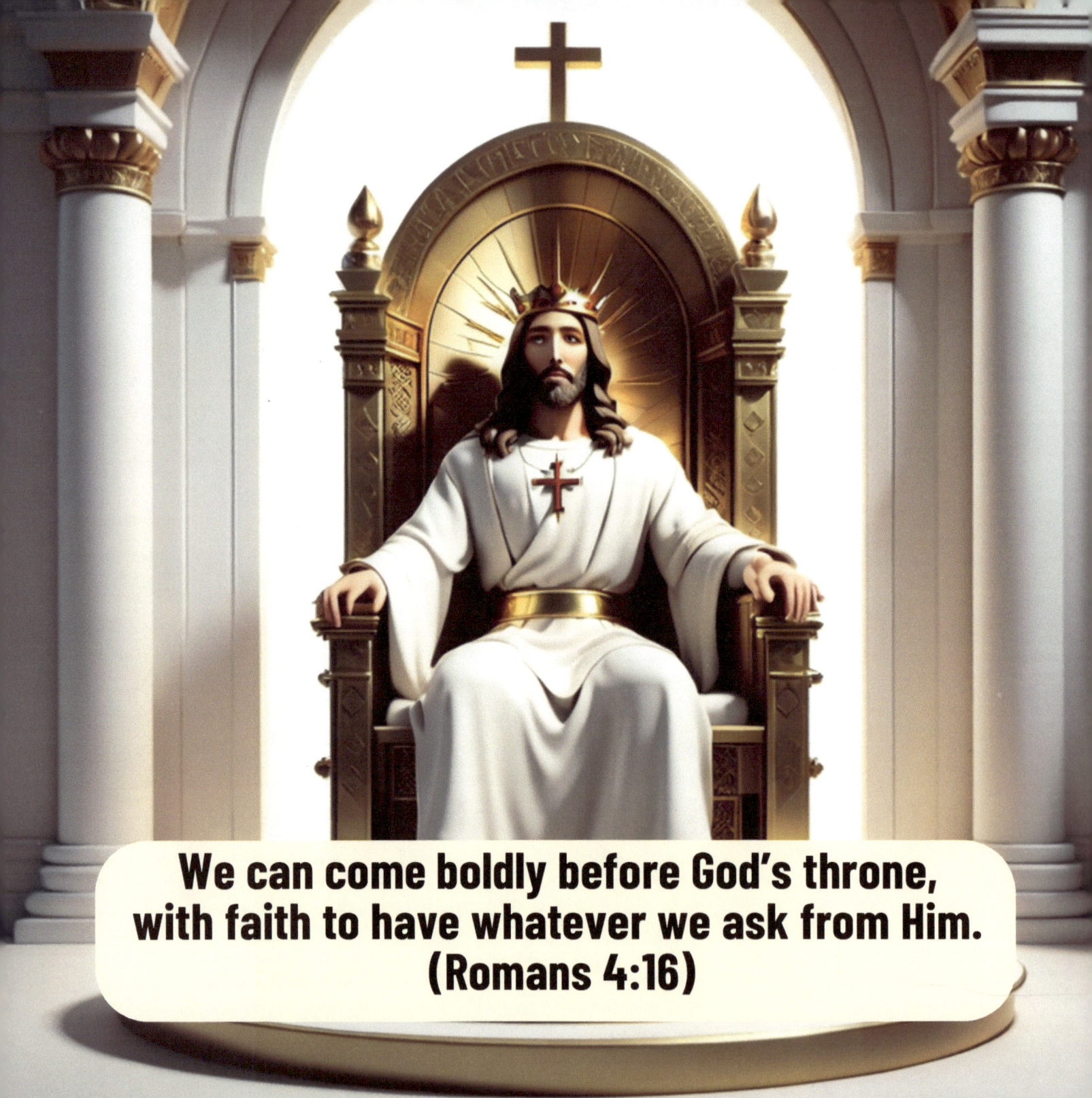

God will judge Satan, and you will get back what he stole and destroyed from you.

We can command the devil to let go of these.
We will see what God planned to happen.
Those who obey will complete God's work.

**The time to act is right away.
We lose the blessings when we don't obey.
There may not be another chance.**

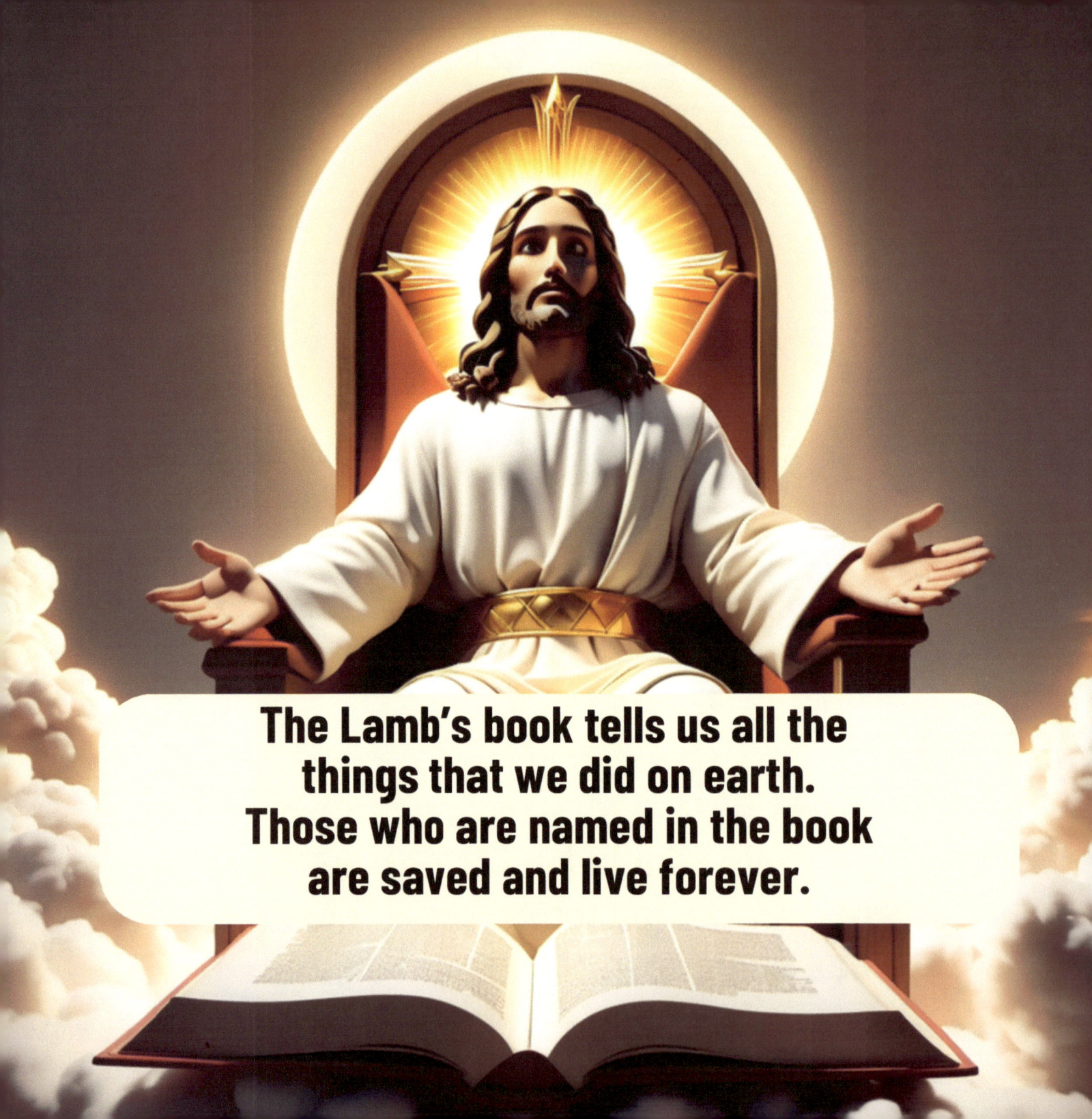

God's judgement will come against the earth. He will judge all the people left when He comes to take His people.

The Father (God), Son (Jesus Christ) and the Holy Spirit work together. They are three in one.

SALVATION PRAYER

God, I know I sinned against you. Forgive me for the wrong that I have done. I believe that Jesus Christ died on the cross for me. That He rose from the grave so that after three days. I can have His long-lasting life. Come into my heart to be my Lord and Savior. I choose to turn away from my sins and I choose to follow you. Lead me to walk with you. Keep me safe and teach me your ways. Stop every bad thing in my life that has an open door to hurt me. Close those doors. Holy Spirit, fill me now in Jesus' name. Amen.

BAPTISM IN THE HOLY SPIRIT

Jesus, you are the one that fills me with Your Spirit. Come Holy Spirit and come into my life and fill me to overflow with Your presence. Come with your fire too. Thank you for the gift of tongues in Jesus' name. Amen.

Open your mouth and let the words come out that God gives you. It will be words that you don't know what they mean. You can ask God what it means. You need to let Him talk through you every day to grow this gift.

He will bring you closer to God and you will know Jesus more. You will have power from God to do great things and know things.

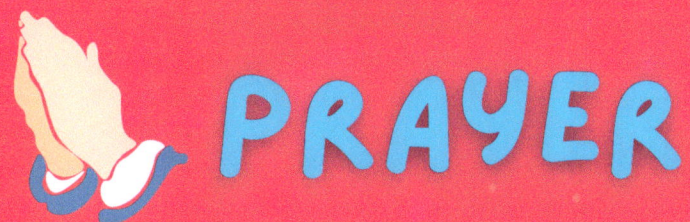

PRAYER

Thank you, Father God, for teaching about your courtroom. Teach me how to use your word to command the devil to let go of my things and to return everything he stole from me. Everything that I lost, I call them to come back in Jesus' name. That Jesus takes them back from the devil for me and that I get 100 fold and 7 times more in Jesus' name. I bind the devil's authority against my finances and loose them into my life in Jesus' name. Amen.

PETITION PRAYER

Father, I come before your you to give my petition. You are a great and awesome God. All majesty, power, and authority are yours. You have given it to Jesus Christ. He has given it to me. King Jesus, I worship before you to have mercy on my life and on behalf of my life. Save us from the enemy's hand. You are the judge of heaven and earth, and I put my trust in you. Hear my cry in Jesus' name. Amen.

DECREE

Father God has given everything into my hands. I am bought by the precious blood of Jesus Christ. I have His life that lasts forever. I have a new life in Jesus. The old man is gone. In Christ, I have all the blessings in heavenly places, and I am seated in heaven. I rule and reign on the earth with power and authority. Nations will come to the Lord and will bow down and worship. I and my family stand strong in the Lord. We will have plenty and more than enough. Our home, families, work, school, and things are blessed. I decree that I have the best home, work, land, and cars. I have everything that the Lord wants to give to me and I can give to others. I will have no lack. I have all the people that God wants me to have in my life. In Jesus' name, I have a good

DECREE CONTINUED

godly property through Christ. My family, home, work, works of my hands, cars, land(s), and school(s), church, ministries, and business(es) are blessed. They will be strong and stable. They will grow in the Lord for His glory. They overflow and all pets are blessed. People will come to know the Lord through me. Miracles, signs, and wonders happen throughout my life. Blessings always come. I will never be afraid. The Lord gives me wisdom, knowledge, and understanding. He gives ideas, plans, help, and money. He gives visions, dreams, and words about the future. Victory will always come. In Jesus' name, the Lord is my Elohim. He is the supreme one. He is my Jehovah Jireh, "the one who provides." He is Jehovah Rapha, "The God who heals." Jehovah

DECREE CONTINUED

Makkadesh, "the Lord who sanctifies." Jehovah NIsseh, "His banner over me is love." Jehovah Tsidkenu, 'The Lord is our Righteousness" Jehovah Shammah, "The Lord is there." Jehovah Rohi, "The Lord my Shepherd." Jehovah Tz'va'ot, "The Lord of Hosts." El Shaddi, "All-sufficient One." He gives us Shalom, which is His peace. El Olam, "The everlasting God." El Roi, "The God who sees." He keeps His covenant forever. The covenant to Abraham, Isaac, and Jacob. I am in covenant with Him. I receive all the promises of God for me and my family up to 1000 generations. We will have success in everything we do. God's favour is with us and people will give into our life. We will stay the head and not the tail. The Lord's hand keeps us from the enemy. That we will not be

DECREE CONTINUED

harmed. That my families and other families will love the Lord and be blessed in Jesus' name. I speak peace over them in Jesus' name. Peace in the home, school, at work, church, wherever I go, and all that I do. Peace over my travels. Peace over the town, the city and country. Open doors to places in your plan and bring me to them to do your will. That all travels will be safe and God's work complete. Wealth, riches, and money are coming to complete the work of God in Jesus' name. Amen.

MESSAGE FROM THE AUTHOR

Thank you for reading this book. I hope you can leave an honest, but helpful review to encourage me to write more books to teach children and adults. The Lord blesses you with all that you do. That you have everything that He wants for you. Use your authority and power in Jesus Christ against Satan and his work. Do not allow him to steal, kill, and destroy your things again. Obey the Lord, Jesus, and the Holy Spirit all the time. The devil will fight us and try to stop us. He will make us lose when we listen to him. Some blessings we get take longer. God will give us better things. We must do our best to walk in God's perfect time and plan. They are the best for us.

OTHER PRODUCTS

Knowing God
How to Hear God's Voice
New Life in Jesus
Loving Israel
God's Gifts/Spiritual Talents
Meeting God
Word Power
Fruit of the Spirit
The Tabernacle
Bride for Jesus
A Life of Prayer
Live Free
Who am I in Jesus
Walk in Love
God's Favor
Man of God
Woman of God
How to Use Money
God's Wisdom
Fasting
See Jerusalem and Bethany
First Fruit Offering
Feast of Trumpets

Day of Atonement
Feast of Tabernacles
Counting the Omer
Festival of Lights
Glory, Presence, and Holy Spirit
Live in God's Presence
Pentecost
See Galilee, Nazareth, and Tiberias
Hear God Speak
Knowing Jesus
Knowing Holy Spirit
A Healthy Life and Healthy Life Work Book
Smokey the Cat
Passover Unleavened Bread
Resurrection Life
The Blessing
Revival
Chelsea Learns Hebrew
Thanksgiving
Give Thanks
Jesus Birth
Loving Jesus: Bride and Groom
Proverbs 31 Woman

OTHER PRODUCTS

ABC of People in the Bible
Colours in the Bible
Breakthroughs
Open Doors
The Seven Spirits of God
Numbers in the Bible
Aglee the Eagle
An Eagle's Life
Chelsea Learns Numbers in Hebrew
ABC's of Faith
Feast of Purim
A Royal Life
Family Day
Family Blessings
Chinese New Year
Loving Jesus for Children
Worship
Pandas
Canada
Celia's Birthday
Animal Stories
Eagles
Fun in West Caribbean

Devotionals
31 Day Devotional

Inspirational/Other
Chelsea's Psalms and Poems
Your Daily Meal: Chelsea's Photo Album
Chelsea's Psalms and Poems2
Travel West Caribbean
Chelsea's Recipes
Chelsea's Psalms and Poems3
Travel to Yellowknife

Puzzle Books
Biblical Puzzle Book Vol 1-5
Bible Puzzles for Young Children Book 1-3
Biblical Puzzle for Children Books 1-5
Chelsea's Bible Puzzles

OTHER PRODUCTS

Teaching Series

How to Hear God's Voice Teaching Guide & Audio Book
Relationship with God, Jesus, Holy Spirit Guide
Knowing God, Jesus, Holy Spirit Guide & Audio Book
Flowing in the Prophetic

Teaching (Non-Sale on my website)
Purim
Passover
Resurrection

BOOK REVIEWS

More books on Amazon, Kobo, and Barnes and Noble, Smashwords, and IngramSpark.
https://chelseak532002550.wordpress.com/

More books on Amazon, Kobo, and Barnes and Noble, Smashwords, and IngramSpark.
https://www.amazon.com/author/chelseakong

Please leave a review and share with friends to help the author continue to write more books to reach more readers. Thank you so much for your support.

Review!

About
CHELSEA KONG

She is a writer, creative arts and digital media artist, skilled administration and certified PCP (Payroll Compliance Professional), and podcaster. Chelsea also served in a variety of roles, from audiovisual, photography, to assisting on the worship team, and ministry team. She also has a passion for families being united.

Chelsea has been a guest on Unity Live Radio, The Lady Tracey Show, and How to Live for Christ and is highly recommended by a Proud Christian blog. She is also a guest blogger. A few of her books have been featured in YourAuthorHub, etc. She graduated from Hotel and Restaurant Management, Digital Media Arts, Office Administration, Payroll Compliance Professional, and experience working with children. Chelsea lives in Toronto, Canada. She mainly writes children's books, stories, bridal writing, poems, lyrics for songs, words of encouragement, blessings, prayers, and jokes. The author of How to Hear the Voice of God, the Bridal Collection, Knowing God, etc. She also has her own Bible Puzzle books and other inspired products. Her podcast channel is called Chelsea K on Anchor, Spotify, and iTunes.

Please check my website to find out more:
https://chelseak532002550.wordpress.com/

www.ingramcontent.com/pod-product-compliance
Lightning Source LLC
Chambersburg PA
CBHW040058160426
43192CB00003B/109